GINA CAMACHO

Financial Literacy for Everyone!

Break The Generational Curse of Being Financially Uneducated!

First published by G. Camacho 2024

Copyright © 2024 by Gina Camacho

All rights reserved. No part of this publication may be reproduced, stored or transmitted in any form or by any means, electronic, mechanical, photocopying, recording, scanning, or otherwise without written permission from the publisher. It is illegal to copy this book, post it to a website, or distribute it by any other means without permission.

Gina Camacho asserts the moral right to be identified as the author of this work.

Gina Camacho has no responsibility for the persistence or accuracy of URLs for external or third-party Internet Websites referred to in this publication and does not guarantee that any content on such Websites is, or will remain, accurate or appropriate.

Designations used by companies to distinguish their products are often claimed as trademarks. All brand names and product names used in this book and on its cover are trade names, service marks, trademarks and registered trademarks of their respective owners. The publishers and the book are not associated with any product or vendor mentioned in this book. None of the companies referenced within the book have endorsed the book.

First edition

This book was professionally typeset on Reedsy.
Find out more at reedsy.com

First and foremost I want to give God all the Glory and Honor for giving me the wisdom to pass on to my readers. I'd also like to thank my husband, and my children for believing in me and for helping me with every part of this book. You guys are my Rock Stars!

Now is the moment of change!

- Prophet Michael Dalton

Contents

1	Introduction	1
2	Before You Grow Up Too Fast	3
3	Parents	6
4	Protect Your Life	8
5	Create An Emergency Fund/Savings	12
6	Investing	14
7	The Rule of 72	18
8	Real Rate of Return	20
9	Beat Inflation	23
10	The Uncle We Don't Know!	25
11	2 Ways To Increase Cash Flow	29
12	Reevaluate Expenses	33
13	Don't Hate The Game Learn The Lingo	36
14	Get Out Of Debt FAST!	38
15	Types Of Asset Accumulation	43
16	Conclusion	48
17	Resources	51

1

Introduction

Hello I just want to say welcome to the Financial Awakening. Let me also say that there will still be a little bit of a learning curve, but if you stick with learning about your finances and use the tools out there to help, you are one step closer to financial freedom. Gone are the days when there was no Financial Literacy for everyone. The world of information can get a little overwhelming, but I'm hoping this short book brings a little bit of clarity in a hurting world. This book will open your eyes to a holistic approach to your Financial House. I'm hoping this book will bring basic financial concepts to you that have been forgotten or hidden from us. Also if I offend anyone because I'm being too forward please forgive me. I'm just trying to shake this into you. HA. I just got the vision of me shaking you to wake you up. Come on, Let's dive right in!

FINANCIAL LITERACY FOR EVERYONE!

2

Before You Grow Up Too Fast

To kids and young adults don't grow up too fast! You have the rest of your lives for that God Willing. Soak up the time of no bills and if you work save up that bag! Help your parents with a bill or two. Trust me it will show you have some sort of responsibility. This will also help you in the long run and give you confidence that you CAN make it! Life will TRY and knock you down but these lessons you learn at home will keep your feet on the ground with your head up.

If you didn't have a chance to learn these lessons at home. That's totally OK. You still have time to learn. Life is all about lessons. When we fail, that's a good thing. Just keep moving forward. Make that your new mindset! Oh and did I tell you already SAVE MORE! When you save make sure you put your savings somewhere you don't have easy access too. Not only do we have to protect our money from the ups and downs of the market, we also have to save it from our 10 fingers. LOL. Let me tell you something the government will not save for you. Your parents have to worry about you and themselves. We have to save on our own. So start NOW!

BEFORE YOU GROW UP TOO FAST

3

Parents

By now we are in a little or a lot of debt. That's ok because like i said before it's NEVER TOO LATE. Start by paying yourself FIRST! The 1st hour you work is for you to save, the rest is for your expenses. Next would be to protect your income for your family. Have you noticed we have insurance for our phones, our tvs, sometimes we insure our travel, but the most important thing is YOU. It's so sad to see families scrabble to find money for burial. It is also hard to put it on someone else to help pay for your burial when they are having a hard time themselves or have their money tied up. Trust me every time we had a family member pass and they were not covered it broke my heart because we could not help the way we wanted too. I want to let you know there is HOPE. There are inexpensive ways to help with that. I will go into more detail later.

It's NEVER too early or LATE to purchase a life policy for your infant or child. Start them young, it is cheaper and it will stay that price for the rest of their lives. You probably do not know what that is now but come back to this section of the book after reading the Protect Your Life Chapter. Now you understand? The best gift is to start them out YOUNG.

Set your Goals. Not setting goals is like trying to get somewhere that you don't know without a GPS. Goals are life's GPS. Set goals for Less than 1 year, 1-5 years, and 5+ years. Absolutely Live Below Your Means! I don't know if you've heard this but I will say it again: People don't plan to fail, We just fail to plan! We are not getting any younger than we are right now!

4

Protect Your Life

OK so by protecting your life I mean your income. If something were to happen to you or your spouse or your child right now in this very instance will your family be ok? Mentally probably not. How about financially? Now this is the part that will offend some people. Go Fund Me or a plate sale or a car wash or any kind of crowdfunding is not life insurance. I hate to burst your bubble, it's not. It's very sad to see that because the family was ill educated or not prepared, or think they have time, whatever the case may be now they are scrambling for funds to bury their loved one. They have zero time to grieve. First the loss of their loved one and now to hustle and find the funds to lay their loved ones to rest. Well here is this thing called life insurance. It is the cheapest and fastest way to make a family whole again. You will have time to grieve. Maybe even take time off work. Or for the momma or poppa who is staying at home and the breadwinner is gone, you will have time to find work, build a business, or even not lose your house. Your payments will NEVER equal the amount they will give you. Please be sure to speak with an insurance professional to figure out what protection is needed.

There are only two types of life insurance and Insurance is determined by a number of things to include height, weight, driving record, job, past health issues, tobacco use, family history, prescribed medication and the main one being age. Remember we are not getting any younger :).

Term means for only a certain period of time. Term insurance also is very, very inexpensive. Term periods can include 5 years, 10 years, 15 years, 20 years or even 30 years depending on the company. Or you can have Term insurance throughout the duration of work. For example like the military we are offered insurance through them, but the moment we leave the military we are no longer covered. When leaving the military we get offered a term Insurance which renews every 5 years. Again we are not getting any younger. LOL!

Permanent means so long as you pay your payment you are covered. Permanent insurance is more expensive but the price of your coverage may stay the same for the life of the policy. Also did you know that you can put money underneath your life insurance. The life insurance policy acts like an umbrella. See tax code 7702.This is the best gift you can give your child, not toys or electronics. Set them up to succeed in life. Their policy will be the same price for the rest of their lives. Then there is this thing about over funding their account. But to keep it simple I'll leave it at that. Speak with an insurance professional.

Here are examples of what an age difference can make. I'm using VGLI one because it is the cheapest and it has the numbers on the website. This one is a term so it increases every 5 years and we will use 300,000 for coverage as an example. I'm going to skip many years so you can see the price difference. You can always check the website as well.

Age	Coverage	Cost
50-54	300,000	99.00
70-74	300,000	678.00
80+	300.000	1350,00

As you can see when we really need the insurance at age 70, 80, and beyond it will not be affordable. Although Term has its purpose, permanent is the way to go. You can't afford to wait!

PROTECT YOUR LIFE

5

Create An Emergency Fund/Savings

If anything had taught us anything it was the time between the end of 2019 and 2022. When the world shut down. It used to be that our emergency fund would be 6 months of income saved up, but that time showed us that we needed at least a year or two saved up.

What is considered an emergency? Well I'll tell you what it's not for (LOL), a coffee from the store, or those shoes that just dropped or even that make-up that was just released. The BUT I NEEEEED IT mentality has to die, or our dreams and future die with it. Your future is more precious than that. It's important that we learn now to live below our means before it's very difficult to dig ourselves out. Trust me it is never, never too late.

Check the emergency calculator websites in the resources below. I also added a savings calculator website.

CREATE AN EMERGENCY FUND/SAVINGS

6

Investing

So there are two types of people: I'll start to invest Now, or Ehhh I can wait to invest Later. Which one are you? Time is our greatest ally or our greatest enemy. When we wait, It's our greatest enemy, because time waits for no one. Have you ever heard of Mr. Invest Now and Mrs. Invest Later? Well let me show you what happened to them. This is for illustration purposes only.

- Mr. I'll Invest Now, invest $3,600 per year for 7 years in an 8% tax-deferred account
- Mrs. Ill Invest Later, decided she wanted to invest 7 years later after her YOLO life. So she starts investing $3,600 per year for 17 years in a 8% tax-deferred account.

INVESTING

Who do you believe got the best deal?

FINANCIAL LITERACY FOR EVERYONE!

Mr. Invest Now				Mrs. Invest Later		
Age	Yearly Contribution	Total Money		Age	Yearly Contribution	Total Money
25	$3,600	$3,888		25		
26	$3,600	$8,087		26		
27	$3,600	$12,622		27		
27	$3,600	$17,520		27		
29	$3,600	$22,809		29		
30	$3,600	$28,522		30		
31	$3,600	$34,629		31		
32		$37,467		32	$3,600	$3,888
33		$40,465		33	$3,600	$8,087
34		$43,702		34	$3,600	$12,622
35		$47,189		35	$3,600	$17,520
36		$50,974		36	$3,600	$22,809
37		$55,052		37	$3,600	$28,522
38		$59,456		38	$3,600	$34,629
39		$64,212		39	$3,600	$41,355
40		$69,349		40	$3,600	$48,52
41		$74,897		41	$3,600	$56,324
42		$80,889		42	$3,600	$64,718
43		$87,360		43	$3,600	$73,783
44		$94,349		44	$3,600	$83,574
45		$101,897		45	$3,600	$94,148
48		$110,048		48	$3,600	$105,567
47		$118,852		47	$3,600	$117,901
48		$128,361		48	$3,600	$131,221
TOTAL CONTRIBUTION: $25,200				TOTAL CONTRIBUTION: $61,200		

OK, So now they are done saving. Who do you think did the smartest thing? Did Mr. Invest Now do it smart or Ms. Invest Later? I know life gets in the way, but what if we were financially educated. What if we could teach our kids these simple concepts? How much better would the world be? Less stressed about money for sure. Did you know that Stress is linked to 6 leading causes of death? So yeah, the less stressed we are the better.

7

The Rule of 72

Here is another concept that is becoming popular. "Albert Einstein's" Rule of 72, but did you know that Luca Pacioli, an Italian mathematician referenced the Rule of 72 in the 1400's. Give credit where credit is due I believe. Albert Einstein did tout Compound Interest rule as 8th Wonder of the World. The Rule of 72 is a formula that is used to figure out how long it's going to take for your money to double. It's pretty cool, if I do say so myself! Take a Look at the example:

THE RULE OF 72

72 /4% = 18 Years		72 / 8% = 9 Years		72 / 12% = 6 Years	
At 4%, money nearly doubles every 18 years		At 8%, nearly doubles every 9 years		At 12%, nearly doubles every 6 years	
Years	Amount	Years	Amount	Years	Amount
29	$10,000	29	$10,000	29	$10,000
47	$20,000	38	$20,000	35	$20,000
65	**$40,000**	47	$40,000	41	$40,000
		56	$80,000	47	$80,000
		65	**$160,000**	53	$160,000
				59	$320,000
				65	**$640,000**

What interest rate would you like in your favor? 12%, Yeah Me too. The difference between 4% VS 12% investing $10,000 is over $600,000. That's the salary of a person who works for 20 years with an annual salary of $30,000, WITHOUT spending any money! Of course this is just an estimate but there is a more accurate equation, but this will do for an estimate. Also this Rule of 72 applies to any debt with an interest rate. Yikes! Try calculating your credit card debt and see how long it will take to double. Scary, Right! Most cards start at 18%. Use that Rule for the interest that our bank gives us for our checking or savings account. What a joke. Let's be generous and say they give us 1% in our checking, calculate that. How many 72 years do we have in our lives? We are lucky if we get one.

8

Real Rate of Return

Now we move on to understanding the real rate of return. First, have you ever heard the rules of one of the richest men in the world Warren Buffet? Rule number #1 Never lose money, and Rule #2 Never forget Rule #1. If you have your money invested in the market, that rule is kind of hard to follow. At least know what you need to get your money back.

This time we will use Mr. Aggressive Investor and Mrs. Conservative Investor. An Aggressive Investor is someone who wants all of the gains and is not worried about the losses. A Conservative Investor finds somewhere he will get a good gain, but they also get a floor. Example: that month the company closes with a %15 gain and that year the company says the client will get %12. Clients only will get the %12 and the rest of the 3% will go to the company. Now if the company goes down -10% the client is guaranteed they never lose money and will receive %0 that month. They didn't lose any money that month.

REAL RATE OF RETURN

Look at the chart below to give a little more understanding.

Example:

	Mr. A	Mrs. C	Are they equal?		Mr. A	Mrs. C
Year 1	+40	+10%	Lets put $100 in the equation	Year 1	$140	$110
Year 2	-20%	+10%		Year 2	$112	$121
Net:	20%	20%		Net:	$112	$121
They are not equal. Who ends up doing better?

Now imagine you are at retirement age and you take a -50% loss of your entire retirement portfolio, let's say $500,000. Could you recover? Probably not. Time would not be on our side. I know I bring up all these questions but it's to open your eyes to these kinds of financial concepts that are kind of brushed under the rug. Can you handle these kinds of losses, and what percentage gain would be required to break even?

Portfolio Investment Loss	Gain Required to Break Even
– 10%	+11%
– 20%	+25%
– 30%	+43%
– 40%	+67%
– 50%	+100%
– 60%	+150%

So know when to pull or move your money around if you're not an aggressive investor. If you are, ride the wave. I'd like to be the first to know where I could get +150% Real Rate of Return.

9

Beat Inflation

What is inflation? In simple terms it's the cost of goods raised over time. So in 2020 the annual inflation rate was 1.2% and in 2022 it was 8.1%. For example average gas prices throughout the US were $2.67/gal. In California the cheapest price was $3.70/gal. In 2024, we are at $4.77/gal and the rest of the world is averaged at $3.55/gal. It's not only gas that has gone up, it is housing, food, everything. I saw a story where in 2020 a man purchased groceries from Walmart for $100, and he ordered the exact same cart of food in 2024 and it came out to over $400. WOW just wow! I know you all have seen these stories.

Since 2020, inflation has gone up 57.7%! What the!!! When dividing that by 23 years the average has been 2.50%. So ask yourself, are we winning or losing in the money game? Wherever you are saving/investing your money make sure you are getting over 5% in interest to beat inflation.

FINANCIAL LITERACY FOR EVERYONE!

10

The Uncle We Don't Know!

FINANCIAL LITERACY FOR EVERYONE!

He used to be the face of the Army, a patriotic symbol of the government and somehow he became the face of our taxes. LOL. There are two things certain in Life, death and taxes.

THE UNCLE WE DON'T KNOW!

That's how our brave men and women in our law enforcement and military and postal services get paid oh and the officials that represent us in government. There are many others but those are the main ones that come to mind right about now.

Know the differences between Tax Now, Tax Deferred and Tax Advantage. These are some examples of the types of accounts in those categories.

- Tax Now - Checking, Savings, CD's Stocks, Mutual Funds
- Tax Deferred - 401k/403(b), IRA/SEP-IRA, Annuity, Pensions
- Tax Advantaged - Roth-IRA, 529 College Savings, Municipal Bonds, Health Savings Account (HSA), Life Insurance, Long Term Care Benefit

Where do you have your money? My suggestion is to put as much money as you can in Tax Advantaged accounts. It's not how much money you make, but how much money you keep. Talk with your tax preparer and they can suggest more for your particular situation. Everyone is different and has different goals. Remember we need a road map to get where we want to go. Set the goals!

FINANCIAL LITERACY FOR EVERYONE!

11

2 Ways To Increase Cash Flow

Contrary to what everyone tells you there are only 2 ways to increase your cash flow.

1. **Spend Less** - Means live below your means. When you are having to use credit cards to eat out! That is above your means. Literally you are pooping your money away. Burning it up! I can show you what you can do with an extra $100.

1. **Earn More** - Sacrifice now so that you can have what you want later. If you have to get more hours, get a second job, or start that business that you've always wanted but fear holds you back. Stop sacrificing your dreams! If you don't do it for you, do it for your kids, your family, your future.

You know when you have a job you work for someone else. You are making someone else's dreams a reality. AhHa! Do you know what the JOB stands for? Just Over Broke, yikes! There is absolutely nothing wrong with a job. We all start there, but that's not the end game. Remember, the money game is just that. A Game. Like monopoly, how many properties can you acquire, how much land, what kind of problems can your business solve. That's all a business is. Finding a problem and fixing it.

So have a plan! The first step is to ALWAYS pay God 1st! Be thankful that we have a job or a business. Next would be to pay yourself. You might as well. You are the one working. Or are we just working to pay the bills? I think NOT! Change your mindset that we pay ourselves the first hour of the day! Think about it: how much could you save in a Tax Advantage account that is giving you a minimum 8%? Say you make $20.00 an hour. That's 600$ a month, that's $7,200 a year, and by the time you hit 61 you have about $115,200. The earlier we start saving the better. Now these numbers are hypothetical. You can save way more, we just need to learn how to. It starts with GOALS! Make more to save more.

2 WAYS TO INCREASE CASH FLOW

FINANCIAL LITERACY FOR EVERYONE!

12

Reevaluate Expenses

Now this is how we are going to save more! Reevaluate where your money is going. Let's start with Tax Season. When you get that money SAVE it! You could be compounding your money to make that $115,000 grow much faster. It really doesn't take much to move the needle. You can have fun, don't get me wrong but save the majority.

Now lets see where our money could be going. What about the electricity bill? Turn the darn lights off when leaving the room. I say that because that was me. LOL. Keep your house warmer or cooler. I know we can't walk around in our birthday suits but if you can, hey it's your cheeks on your seats LOL. If it's colder, bundle up, turn that heat down. That's the thing about it being cold we can always layer. Wear socks in the house or pantuflas. That's Spanish for house slippers :D. Stop going to Starbucks and start making your coffee at home. This can save bookoo bucks. Don't be too bougie for coupons. You have GOALS! Stop buying a new car every year. Sorry! Someone had to tell me LOL. Use discounts. Play the free video games. Check your phone for monthly subscriptions. If they are not for work, cancel the subscriptions. Check your online subscriptions/Magazine subscriptions. I can't tell you how many subscriptions I was being charged for that I had forgotten or even knew about. Talk about a face smack! Cancel the gym membership that you don't use. Remember Money Goals. Last but definitely not the least, every six months revise your home and auto insurance. I know you might be loyal to Juan from State Farm, but he might not be able to give you the best rate at the time. So shop around, trust me they will fight for your business.

REEVALUATE EXPENSES

13

Don't Hate The Game Learn The Lingo

- What's an Asset? Assets put money in your pocket. They are worth something. Examples: Everything in your Checking, Savings, Cash, Retirement accounts, Brokerage accounts, Your home (if paid off), Vehicles, Jewelry and furniture, Small business.

- What is Liability? Liabilities take money out of your pocket. They have a claim on your assets. Examples: Mortgages, Car loans, Student loans, Credit Card debt, and Accounts payable.

- What is Net Worth? Net Worth is just your Assets – Liabilities = Net Worth. If your Assets are more than your Liabilities then you have a positive net worth and are pretty good at paying your debts on time. Same goes for the opposite. If your Liabilities are greater than your Assets then you have a negative net worth. Which could also mean you have a hard time paying your debts.

Now is where you would ask yourself if what you are bringing in is more than your expenses. How do you calculate your monthly cash flow? Well here is the formula.

Total Income – Total Asset – Total Liability – Total Monthly = Monthly
Contribution Contribution Expenses Cash Flow

You will probably need to read this again because it's important: Knowledge is Power, IF you put that knowledge to use! So what are you going to do with this knowledge? I hope you say take a look at your finances. :)

14

Get Out Of Debt FAST!

So most of America is in some kind of debt. To be exact as a whole the US is $1.115 Trillion Dollars in Credit Card debt. If you're not in CC debt. Pat yourself on the back! Give yourself a high five! Jump for Joy, Literally! You are better off than most Americans. Don't get me wrong, CC's are good. They help build credit, they can be used to start your own business and maintain one. Once the CC is used, lets just say to build credit. Then once the cycle has ended pay it off. Just to show that you can pay your bills.

Remember the Rule of 72 I was telling you about for your saving interest rate. Well the same Rule applies to CC/Loan/Mortgage debt. For example: say you get a credit card, on average, the starting interest rate is 18%. 72/18 = 4 years. So every 4 years if that balance is not paid off it will have doubled, Crazy I know! If you are paying the minimum on a CC it will keep you in the hole forever! Or at least for years. So if you can pay an extra $20 to $40 dollars or even $100. You will pay that CC off so much sooner. Also did you know that your CC statement shows you how long it will take to pay off your CC if you are just paying the minimum? Well now you do. So if you have a CC with the amount of

$20,000 at an 18% interest rate, and you only pay the minimum, it will take you over 94 Months to pay off. Insert picture here, Mind blown!

So let's talk about the Debt Snowball Method or Debt Roll Up! Remember all that money you found when you went over your living expenses, and you cut out unnecessary expenses. So you found an extra $100. Make a list of all of your debt from greatest to least. With that extra $100 you found, apply it to the smallest debt first. If you google debt snowball calculators you can input your creditors there. I have included some I think are excellent in the resources below. In simplest terms, once you finish paying the smallest debt, you would use the $100 + previous payment on the next payment, and once that one is paid off then that whole previous payment will be added to the next minimum on your list, and so on. You will knock out your debt in no time. For example, we will say a CC with a balance of $150 with an interest rate of 28% and the minimum monthly payment is $10 would have taken you 19 months to pay off but since you are adding the $100 + 10 it's going to take you 2 months to pay off that CC debt. Isn't that exciting! I know huh! ;) Then your next debt is another CC with a balance of $400 with an interest rate of 19% with a minimum payment of $25 would have taken you 19 months to pay off. When you add the $110 + $25 = 135 that CC will be paid in less than 3 months. Are you getting the idea? Now you add that $135 to the next bill. I know you get the idea now. The idea is to use the previous bills money on the next bill, NOT to say you have extra money. It takes discipline for anything we want in life, but trust me it will get easier and you will learn to love it. You know how I know because that was me and my husband. We did it! Before I met my husband he was in over $80,000 in debt. It took him less than 5 years to get out of debt. So if we can do it I know you can too! My problem was spending $500 on an outfit for one night of fun. Aye! If I could tell my younger self what I know now, I would have gotten where

GET OUT OF DEBT FAST!

I wanted to be faster. Funny thing is we dont look at what we spend! When I came into the house with all the bags, my sister was like what the heck! How much did you spend? I told her IDK. She told me to give her the receipt because I didn't want to know what I spent. When it was brought to my attention I was blown away. I didn't use credit but I did burn through my check like I didn't have a future to save for.

In the resources below there is an awesome Debt Roll Up or Snowball Calculator. I also added a site to tell you how long it will take to pay off a CC if you pay the minimum. If you also add a little bit of more than the minimum it will show you how much faster it will take to pay that same CC off. Please use it. None of your information is saved, it is just a calculator. Remember Knowledge is power, IF you put that knowledge to use. :D Yes I will beat a dead horse! Also no horses were hurt in this process! LOL. Don't come at me.

FINANCIAL LITERACY FOR EVERYONE!

15

Types Of Asset Accumulation

Ok by now we might have a little bit more handle on some of the financial concepts, and trust me you will get it down. It just takes a little bit of practice, I have faith in you! So while we are saving, creating an emergency fund, and getting down our debt, we have to think about our retirement. It's ok, just take a deep breath. YOU GOT THIS!

Some of the ways we can accumulate our assets are offered through our jobs, and some are on our own. This will be nice and quick. Just a little bit of digging on the net will be helpful so you are not so overwhelmed right now.

- Company Pension - Went out of style Mostly Military, Some Government associations. I remember when it was almost my mothers time to retire and they let her go before that. It was super sad to see. Now, you have no control on what you're going to get. It's based on the number of years of service and your average salary during the last few years of employment.

- Defined Contribution Plans - 401k, TSP, 403(b) or IRAs. These are funded by your pre-tax dollars from your work paycheck. And in many instances you can only contribute to those accounts while you are working for said company. You are responsible for choosing how much you want to contribute as well as where you want to invest. You can be aggressive with your portfolio or conservative. Some companies may "match" what you are contributing. With these types of accounts comes RMD's (Required Minimum Distributions) When you turn 72 the government is going to tell you you have to withdraw a certain amount of money from your accounts. If you do not you will be hit with a 25% penalty along with whatever tax bracket you are in. For example 33% tax bracket. So even if you don't need the money you will have to withdraw from your account and that money is income. So remember these ages:

Prior to 59 ½ if you withdraw, you will be penalized 10% plus it is taxed as ordinary income.

Over 59 ½ you withdraw and you are just taxed as ordinary income.

Over 73 if you have not withdrawn, you are going to be required to withdraw whatever percent that is mandated and if the RMD is not met you will be Penalized 25%. That will also be taxed as ordinary income.

TYPES OF ASSET ACCUMULATION

The RMDs with Money example:

This is an example if you took out $20,000 at the following ages stated above. How much will the penalty, tax, and how much would you get out of that $20,000. We will say your tax bracket is 30% in this example and you were required to withdraw $40,000.

Age	Penalty	Tax	Net $
50	$2000	$6000	$12000
60	$0	$6000	$14000
75	$5000 RMD Penalty	$6000	$9000

RMD is a very important concept because if we forget to take out the RMD we will again burn a lot of money, and we really didn't have to if we knew these basic concepts.

- So-So Security - I mean Social Security :D This is very important as well. It was never meant to be a stand alone retirement plan. It was meant to supplement your other retirement programs. I know watching my mother go through this first hand that no one could live off of SSI alone. There is a program out there that can help you with your goals and your quarters and all that jazz. There are so, so , so many rules to this game. Use the source in the resource below to help maximize your Social Security Benefits. It could cost you thousands of dollars.

- Personal Savings - This is another very important tool to use in your financial toolbox. We need to start thinking about self-funding our own retirement. The GOV will now come and save you. These little checks that they throw at us did not do us any favors. So Roth IRA, Cash Value Life Ins, Stocks, Mutual Funds are just a few examples of how you can add to your financial portfolio.

There are many ways you can self fund your retirement, and there are many free classes you can attend that financial professionals can help you with.

TYPES OF ASSET ACCUMULATION

16

Conclusion

When I was introduced to these concepts over 16 years ago they changed the trajectory of how my life was going. We were not taught any of these financial concepts in school or by our family because they too didn't know any better. I believe at the time of this writing some schools are adding it as an elective in school. One of my friends' daughters said she didn't want to take it because she didn't want that class to bring her GPA down. Let your babies know that it is nothing to be scared about, and this is life. Lets lead by example and be the one in our family that breaks the financial education generational curse. Just know even in college getting a degree in financial studies these concepts are not taught. My friend who has their Doctorate Degree also said they received their degree and not one of these were mentioned. They went to school all those years and not once were these concepts introduced! WOW. I guess it's learn as you go, and unfortunately some never get the message. So if this short book helps just one person my heart would be filled. I just want to reach one

CONCLUSION

person at a time.

All these concepts are for educational purposes only. Further research is needed as each person's financial situation is different. Not one person is the same. Everyone has different goals.

If you found this book to be helpful in any way, it would mean the world to me to know that this little book was able to help to awaken a sleeping giant. Even if it was just one concept that helped, could you do me a huge favor and leave a favorable review. Reviews are worth their weight in gold. And if it made you LOL please insert that too. I love to make people laugh, even though this is a serious topic. Life is too short to stress when things can be fixed. My heart goes out to each and everyone of you and know that people care.

With Love,
    A Girl Born and Raised in Texas and Living in Cali.

FINANCIAL LITERACY FOR EVERYONE!

17

Resources

Protect Your Life:

Insneighbor. (2023, March 17). **GoFundMe vs. Life Insurance**: What You Should Know. Insurance Neighbor. https://www.insuranceneighbor.com/gofundme-vs-life-insurance-what-you-should-know/#

Veterans' Group Life Insurance (VGLI) | Veterans Affairs. (2023, March 1). Veterans Affairs. https://www.va.gov/life-insurance/options-eligibility/vgli/

Slmainc. (2022b, March 30). **The science of STRESS.** SLMA. https://www.slma.cc/the-science-of-stress/

Horton, C. (2023, August 11). **IRS tax Code 7702: How it affects your life insurance policy.** Forbes Advisor. https://www.forbes.com/advi

sor/life-insurance/tax-code-7702-plan/#

Emergency Fund/ Savings:

Horton, C. (2023a, July 19). **Emergency Fund calculator.** Forbes Advisor. https://www.forbes.com/advisor/banking/emergency-fund-calculator/

SAVINGS CALCULATOR – WSB. (n.d.). https://worldsystembuilder.com/savings-calculator/

Rule of 72:

What is the Finance Rule of 72? | Double Your Money | Napkin Finance. (2020b, December 29). Napkin Finance. https://napkinfinance.com/napkin/rule-of-72/

Inflation:

Srinivasan, H. (2024, June 12). **U.S. inflation rate by year: 1929 to 2024.** Investopedia. https://www.investopedia.com/inflation-rate-by-year-7253832

Movement, Q.-. P. a. P. W. (2023, January 3). **Is inflation high compared to years past?** Breaking down inflation rates by year. Forbes. https://www.forbes.com/sites/qai/2023/01/02/is-inflation-high-compared-to-years-past-breaking-down-inflation-rates-by-year/

Retail gasoline prices rose across the United States in 2021 as driving increased - U.S. Energy Information Administration (EIA). (n.d.-b). https://www.eia.gov/todayinenergy/detail.php?id=50758#

RESOURCES

The Uncle We Don't Know:

Taxable income | Internal Revenue Service. (n.d.). https://www.irs.gov/filing/taxable-income#

Don't Hate The Game Learn The Lingo

Ganti, A. (2024, June 20). **Net Worth: What it is and how to Calculate it**. Investopedia. https://www.investopedia.com/terms/n/networth.asp#

Get Out Of Debt Fast

Schulz, M. (2024, June 13). **2024 Credit Card Debt Statistics**. LendingTree. https://www.lendingtree.com/credit-cards/study/credit-card-debt-statistics/

Credit card payoff calculator. (n.d.). Experian. https://www.experian.com/blogs/ask-experian/credit-card-payoff-calculator/

Snowball debt Payoff Calculator. (n.d.). https://www.calculators.org/debt/accelerated-payoff.php

Debt Roll-Up Calculator – WSB. (n.d.). https://worldsystembuilder.com/debt-rollup-calculator/

Asset Accumulation:

Retirement plan and IRA Required Minimum Distributions FAQs | Internal Revenue Service. (n.d.-b). https://www.irs.gov/retirement-plans/retirement-plan-and-ira-required-minimum-distributions-faqs

RSSA. (2024, June 28). **Social Security advisors. Maximize your benefits.** https://rssa.com/

www.ingramcontent.com/pod-product-compliance
Lightning Source LLC
Chambersburg PA
CBHW071958210526
45479CB00003B/989